Published by
SPLH Publishing
P.O. Box 805624
Chicago, IL 60601

Printed in the United States of America

Library of Congress Cataloging-in-Publication Data

ISBN 978-0-9765330-0-9

Artwork by Leslie Bardo
Photography by Dan Dry
Cover by Gameplan

Warning – Disclaimer
The purpose of this book is to educate and entertain. The author or publisher does not guarantee that anyone following the ideas, tips, suggestions, techniques or strategies will become successful. The author and publisher shall have neither liability or responsibility to anyone with respect to any loss or damage caused, or alleged to be caused, directly or indirectly by the information contained in this book.

As a young incoming freshman at the University of Illinois, Stephen made a special effort to take the younger players under his wing and help them make the adjustment from high school to college. Stephen's leadership qualities were and still are what make him stand out! His knowledge of what it takes to be successful is something that many can learn from.

Tom Michael
Assistant Athletic Director for Academic Affairs
University of Illinois

Stephen Bardo was the type of basketball player that every coach and every official would like to have on the floor. His hard-nosed and tenacious play positively influenced his teammates and opponents alike.

He was the consummate professional—the type of individual that parents wish they could take home and have as their son. He was a role model in his playing days—he remains a role model today.

Stephen has always wanted to make the game of basketball better, and he continues to do that in his current positions as he works with young people and as a commentator for ESPN and Illini basketball.

Stephen Bardo is one of my all-time favorite basketball players, as well as one of my all-time favorite people.

Ed Hightower – Top NCAA Men's Basketball Referee /
Superintendent Edwardsville Illinois school district

Stephen came in and inspired our students to achieve their goals within our new reading and math program. Long after his presentation students still remind my staff of his inspirational stories.

Stacy Bobo – Principal Zela Davis Elementary School, Hawthorne California

ACKNOWLEDGMENTS

To my mother Lana Bardo, and my father Harold Bardo for always pushing me to be my best and always believing in me. I love you both very much. To Stephen Paul and Landon for showing me miracles happen everyday! To Helen and Craig for your unending love and support.

To the Bryson's, Henry's, and Harper's thank you for adding to my extended family.

Thank you Jim Berry for being a great mentor and a better friend.

To my entire extended network that reaches around the globe, I say thank you!!!

HOW TO MAKE THE LEAGUE WITHOUT PICKING UP THE ROCK

THE ULTIMATE TEENAGE SUCCES GUIDE

STEPHEN BARDO

Table of Contents

How to Make the League Without Picking Up the Rock

IN THE BEGINNING...

Little did I know when I was playing every sport I could during my youth that I was also getting life training. Most of the basic structures people experience (school, job, church, community, etc.) mirror sports. In sports, you have coaches and players. In school, you have teachers and students. On the job, you have bosses and employees.

Sports involvement is one of the best experiences you can have to prepare for life.

However, far too many student athletes (with their parents' blessing) want to pursue an athletic career over more traditional professions (lawyers, doctors, managers, etc.) than are chosen. Statistics show only 0.8 percent of high school student athletes receive a full athletic scholarship to a college or university. That means EVERYONE else must choose another career path whether they want to or not. The numbers show you must have a backup plan if one of your goals is to play professional sports.

How to Make the League Without Picking Up the Rock is my collection of thoughts and experiences on high achievement and success strategies for young people. If you are reading this book, you have the ability to live your dreams and accomplish more than you thought possible.

I love the subject of high achievement because my parents stressed it in everyday life and expected my older brother, older sister, and me to do our part. From the academic side, both parents were demanding when it came to achievement in school. My father with his Ph.D. in educational psychology, and my mother, with her bachelor's degree in microbiology, didn't compromise when it came to schoolwork: no grades, no ball-- simple as that!

In addition to the strong academic setting, I reaped the benefits of being the youngest of three student athletes at the college level in the same house. My father played basketball and ran track and cross country at Southern Illinois University (SIU). My brother played basketball at Indiana University and The Citadel. My sister played basketball at John A. Logan Junior College. And on the tennis court and golf course my Mom will give you a run for your money! Competition permeated our house, which made constant involvement in sports mandatory!

I can remember always having to do my best just to keep up with everyone else. Our extended family, which included several families in Carbondale, was athletic and competitive as well. I was the youngest of all of the kids, so every day was an adventure for me. Just making little improvements was a huge deal for me and laid the groundwork for my attitude of constantly striving for greatness.

When I played college basketball at the University of Illinois, we constantly referred to "The League." For us, this meant the NBA; for the football players, it meant the NFL; and for track and field athletes, it meant the Olympics! Generally speaking, anyone that mentioned "The League" referred to the next level or the professional level.

When I played in the CBA (the minor league of the NBA), we talked about "The League" constantly. We rode on buses for what seemed like days at a time, and taking three small planes (known as "puddle-jumpers") for one game really set the stage for fantasizing about "The League." Staying in motels instead of the Ritz Carlton or the Four Seasons made me often wonder what it was like on the other side.

My college teammates were playing in the NBA (league) at the time, and I would ask them constantly how it felt, what was it like, how it was to have that kind of money, and all of the other questions that came to mind.

After a couple of years of playing in the CBA and overseas, I got to experience the League for myself. I made the opening day roster for the Dallas Mavericks in my third season! I can't begin to explain how happy and proud I was to accomplish one of my dreams.

During my brief stints in the NBA, I was fortunate enough to play with some outstanding players and citizens. Two that come to mind are Joe Dumars and Mark West. Through Mark and Joe's experiences, I learned that everyone has the ability to do whatever it is they put their minds to! There are unlimited opportunities for you to be the best in any field you choose. You may not be born with talent to play sports well or be able to sing like Beyonce, but God gives all of us something very special to work with. It's your job to find out what that is. Believe it or not, you do SOMETHING as good as or better than anyone else does! It's not important if you don't know the answer today. Just keep asking yourself what you can do better than anyone else.

This book is designed to help you achieve your goals through time-tested ideas that are common among high achievers. This book will also give you some things to think about and prepare for along your path to success in whatever area you desire.

I have found that EVERYONE has his or her own League! Whether you are studying to be a doctor, lawyer, accountant, teacher, musician, graphic artist, or whatever your talent, everybody has a journey, and that journey announces to the world "I'm in the League"!

ONE

Backup Plan

CONTRARY TO WHAT IS SEEN AND PUT OUT THERE... YOU MUST HAVE A PLAN B... LIFE IS TOO UNPREDICTABLE TO COUNT ON ONE ROUTE TO ENSURE SUCCESS....

- Stephen Bardo

-       There are nearly 1 million high school football players and 550,000 basketball players. Of that number, 250 make it to the NFL and 50 make it to the NBA.

-       Less than 3 percent of college seniors will play one year in professional basketball.

-       The odds of a high school football player making it to the pros at all, let alone having a career, are roughly 6,000 to 1; the odds for a high school basketball player are 10,000 to 1.

-       In the music industry, 75% of the songs you hear on the radio or see in music videos lose money, while a lot of these artists flame out after one song or album.

These statistics show that you must develop multiple plans if you plan on playing professional sports or want a career in the music industry.

The numbers don't lie. But I'm not all gloom and doom so I would like to talk about someone I know that did beat the odds. His name is Kendall Gill; he was very fortunate come from a solid family situation with two loving parents and a good family support system.

Kendall grew up in Matteson, Illinois, a southern suburb of Chicago. He always knew what he wanted to do. He was this "string bean," so skinny he could hula-hoop a cheerio!

But he worked on his skills and was a strong player, despite being really thin in high school.

When Kendall got to college, his focus was even sharper. You see, Kendall patterned himself after one of the best players ever. He would study this player so much, many people thought his game resembled that of his role model. Kendall always knew that he needed to get stronger if he was going to accomplish his dream of playing in the NBA, so during the summer between his sophomore and junior year he gained 25 pounds of pure muscle! While many of the students at school were watching TV or hanging out, Kendall would take breaks during his studies and do push-ups, sit-ups, and wall sits to strengthen his legs. Then, during the team weight-room sessions, he worked out like his life depended on it. He wanted to get stronger so badly because he knew that was one of the few things keeping him from his goal to star in the NBA. His role model, by the way, was none other than Michael Jordan!

Kendall was the #5 pick in the 1990 NBA draft and is still playing, having just completed his 14th season. Quite an accomplishment for the skinny kid from Matteson.

I share the story about Kendall because he is one of the few who make it in professional sports. Today it's not enough for young people to think they can make it in sports or the music industry.

"[I CAN'T] ARE WORDS THAT HAVE NEVER BEEN IN MY VOCABULARY. I BELIEVE IN ME MORE THAN ANYTHING IN THIS WORLD" - WILMA RUDOLPH

You need to have a backup plan just in case things don't work out the way you want them to, because statistics show they may not! Now I'm not saying don't go after your dreams. By all means, go after them with as much intensity as you can, but realize that very few people actually experience professional sports.

A backup plan will ensure you have a bright and productive future. There are so many different areas of interest that you can pursue. I have one request of you, and that's to find what you LOVE, not like, but LOVE to do. You see, when you start working, it's best to really enjoy what you do because most adults spend more time working than anything else! So if you have to devote the most time to work, make it something you can excel in and really enjoy.

In today's world, despite recent job losses, there is no better time in history for young people to succeed! With the Internet and a global economy, the opportunities for young people are endless. There are far more stories of young people finding success in areas outside of sports and entertainment than within them. I know sports and entertainment are hot fields and look like so much fun. I can't argue with that, and I know from my own playing career that they are very cool and very exciting. But what I've discovered is there are many opportunities within the sports and entertainment industry that allow you to be close to the action yet in a much more secure area that allows far more longevity than being participants.

Now I must warn you, nothing worth having is easy. This is not a quick-fix type of book, because true success takes time and effort. There are no shortcuts to success like some people believe. With any true, long-term success, you MUST pay the price upfront and in full before you reap the benefits. It takes time to learn the area that you are in, develop the skills to do the job, and see how to dominate and be a top performer in your industry.

But don't get discouraged. There is good news! All of us have access to something that will give us the foundation we need to succeed. I think you know what it is. It's getting an ***education***.

Education is the one equalizer that EVERYONE has access to! Education is the first step or the foundation that any successful person builds on. Education comes in many different forms--the classroom, travel, and on-the-job training are a few examples.

But whichever one fits you best, you must have it if you want to make The League.

Challenge yourself to be the very best in the classroom because you MUST compete in class just like you would in sports. Challenge yourself to learn how to learn, not just to memorize and take a test. But really learn and understand what you need to because this will benefit you for the rest of your life. Remember, you are part of a global economy and you have to compete against people your age around the world, not just here in the United States.

Write down three areas/subjects of interest to you.

1. _____

_____

2. _____

_____

3. _____

_____

Write down three career choices from your areas of interest, and explain how education will assist you in achieving your career goals.

1. _____

_____

2. _____

_____

3. _____

Chapter 2

Setting Goals

"SET YOUR GOALS HIGH, AND DON'T STOP
TILL YOU GET THERE"

Bo Jackson

Throughout my life, I have been involved in sports in some way.
I have been on baseball, basketball, football, and track teams
throughout my 30 years of participating in sports. As I look back
on these experiences, I notice that the better teams all did one
thing at the beginning of the season. THEY ALL SET GOALS!

Whether it was a goal to win the conference, advance to the state
tournament, score a certain number of points, or hold opponents
to a low score, goals guide us in the direction of success.

It seems obvious that we all need goals to give us direction and
focus in achieving our goals, but very few people, when asked,
could give you a clear picture of their goals.

Goals act as a compass to guide you to achieve what you want. There are three parts in setting and achieving goals. First, you must decide what you want, and be specific. Second, you must write the goals down and keep them close to where you can see and review them every day. Third, you must take action and plan steps to take to achieve your goals.

Clarity, or being exactly sure about what your goals are, is very important. The mind is an amazing tool when used properly, especially in the goal- setting area. When you are clear about what it is you want to achieve, nothing can stop you or your team from achieving it.

Have you ever dreamed something and then later realized that you were doing what you dreamed about? This is called déjà vu. This same power we all have will allow you to visualize your goals. If you use this with the action you need to take to work on your goals, you can accomplish anything and everything you want! But remember, you must be very specific in what it is you want to achieve.

During my last year in pro basketball, I played with Toshiba, a team that in 30 years had never reached the playoffs before I got there. In my first season with my U.S. teammate Fred Lewis, we reached the semifinals, losing to Toyota. All of my Japanese teammates were happy because they had never experienced winning before, but Fred and I had other plans.

We reached the finals each of the next two seasons but lost both times to league powerhouse Isuzu. At the beginning of my final season, my team would meet with a trained sports therapist, and he would ask us to visualize how we would react when we won the championship.

Notice I said, "When we won," not "IF we won." It's very important for you to realize the power of your mind. You have to already know and believe in your mind that you will accomplish what you want before you can do it!

In the final game of the league championship, we knew with 5 minutes left in the game we were going to be champions because we had a huge lead. As the last few seconds ticked off the clock and the celebration began, my arms went straight up in the air, my head down toward the floor, with the biggest smile on my face that I could muster!

When the team therapist at the beginning of the season asked us to close our eyes and visualize how we would react WHEN we won the championship, my arms were straight up in the air and my head went down toward the floor, and I had a huge smile on my face! This is a perfect example of how important clarity is to the success of achieving your goals.

When you write down your goals, they change from being dreams to being goals. Everybody has dreams, but how many of us write them down and review them every day? If you do this, you will put yourself in the top 3 percent of people in the United States who achieve greatness. Having your goals close by at ALL times will ensure you stay focused on what's important. When you review your goals every day, say them out loud, and think about them, you will be blazing a path to greatness that is set by YOU!

You will be amazed at what you can get done just thinking about your goals every day. When you review them, you may need to change them for different situations. That's fine. Just make the adjustment, and keep moving forward.

One way to keep your goals close is to have two copies of them, one to hang somewhere and look at every day (such as on your bedroom mirror, bathroom door, refrigerator door, etc.) and a smaller copy that fits in your wallet or purse.

Being able to pull out the second copy during the day will help keep you on track and make the right decisions and put you one step closer to what you want.

Start off with smaller goals. When you reach them, it will give you momentum and a good feeling about yourself that will allow you to tackle bigger ones later on. You don't want to start off with goals that are too hard to achieve. This will only frustrate you and stop you before you reach your destination.

Clarity and writing down goals are very important, but the last and the hardest step is taking action. Many people know what they want and even write it down, but most of us either lack the motivation to get going or don't know how to put the plan into action.

I believe the lack of motivation comes from a lack of desire behind the goal. I've always tried to have goals that really meant something to me. I always dreamed of playing in the NBA when I was a kid. That's what gave me the motivation to run back and forth a mile each way to the basketball court to play and work on my game. That's why, even after getting beat most of the time growing up playing against older kids I would still want to play, because that's what I dreamed about. There was no stopping me once I knew that's what I wanted, dreamed, and loved to do!

"I WANTED TO BE THE GREATEST HITTER WHO EVER LIVED. A MAN HAS TO HAVE GOALS – FOR A DAY, FOR A LIFETIME. AND THAT WAS MINE." - TED WILLIAMS

If you have struggled with math in the past and you set a goal to get an "A" in algebra, that goal may seem unrealistic. But if, as part of your action plan, you wrote down (1) "meet with a tutor once or twice a week," (2) "spend 30 to 45 minutes four nights a week on algebra," and (3) "ask the teacher for ways to get extra credit," the goal seems within reach because you can see yourself doing these smaller steps throughout the school year.

There's a saying by Bryan Tracy, one of my favorite authors, about attacking big projects or goals: "How do you eat an elephant? One bite at a time!" Once you see how to break your goal down into smaller steps, it's easier to see how you can be successful. Ask a parent, teacher, school counselor, aunt, uncle, or any other adult you trust to help you break down your goals. This way someone else can help you check your progress using these steps to see how close you are to achieving your goal.

So, first be exactly sure of what it is you want to achieve, then write out an action/success plan, take action on your plans every day, and get up every morning and review your goals. Be proud that you have started on a journey that will bring you more happiness, success, and freedom than you ever thought was possible!

Write down five goals you would like to accomplish.

1.

_____

2.

_____

3.

_____

4.

_____

5.

_____

Break down and list three steps per goal that will help you achieve them.

1.

_____

_____

_____

2.

_____

_____

_____

3.

_____

_____

4.

_____

_____

_____

5.

_____

_____

_____

Make a written plan; take steps toward your goals with the help of parents, teachers, and coaches; and set a time for the goals' completion.

Chapter 3

Positive Mental Attitude

My thoughts before a big race are usually pretty simple. I tell myself: Get out of the blocks, run your race, stay relaxed. If you run your race, you'll win.... Channel your energy. Focus.
-Carl Lewis

Do you notice some classmates at school seem to be more popular than others? The students' teachers seem to like and who get better grades? Or the young men or women everyone just likes to be around? Chances are, the students who stand out and attract people to them are students with a positive mental attitude!

Having a positive attitude and high self-esteem are MUSTS if you want to be successful at anything! Our attitudes set the stage for what will happen in our lives and give us fuel to go after what we want.

Great attitude, great results; fair attitude, fair results; bad attitude, bad results. We are the captains of our own team, and our futures will be molded by our attitudes.

Have you ever taken a test in one of your weaker subjects and said to yourself, "Oh man, I'm gonna flunk this test, I just know it"? Or, "I'm so nervous, and this free throw is for the game; I hope it goes in"? In both cases, chances are you achieved the outcome you were striving for. If you set yourself up to fail in your mind, you will fail almost every time.

Your mental attitude is a two-way street: You can either expect to succeed or expect to fail. There are times when you expect to succeed and don't and other times when you think you will fail and actually succeed. My experiences have shown me that most times your attitude will have a huge impact on the outcome of everything you do.

There will be many times when challenges and obstacles get in your way and things don't work out. Life is a series of sunny days when things go well and storms when things don't go so well. But the sooner you understand this and accept it, the sooner you will be able to use your positive attitude to make these setbacks learning lessons and move on.

When I was growing up, my parents used to get on my case when I would walk around the house in a bad mood. They taught me at an early age that even if things weren't going the way you want them to, a bad attitude would not change the situation. But if you remain positive and upbeat, things will turn for the better much faster than you would expect.

Author Dennis Kimbro states in his book *Think and Grow Rich: A Black Choice*, "It's the attitude that you have toward yourself that will determine your attitude toward the world"! The main difference between successful students and students who struggle is the successful ones BELIEVE they can accomplish whatever they set their minds to. We all have the ability to achieve greatness; we just have to SNATCH it!

I used to pattern my game after a certain professional basketball player. He was a tall point guard, could pass really well, and seemed to command respect everywhere he played. In his first year in the NBA, he led the Los Angeles Lakers to a championship when he played center in game 6 of the NBA finals against the Philadelphia Sixers.

With the Lakers' star center Kareem Abdul-Jabbar out with an ankle injury, Magic Johnson stepped up big-time with 46 points in winning the NBA championship in his 1st season! As great a player as Magic Johnson was in becoming a soon-to-be hall-of-famer and being named one of the top 50 players of all time, he has become an even better businessman after his playing days were over. He is fast approaching the billion-dollar mark with his businesses, and he has done all this while being HIV-positive!

People live long and relatively normal lives with HIV now, but in the early 1990s, when Magic was diagnosed, many people believed

" A COLLEGE STUDENT'S CONCENTRATION LEVEL IS (5) MINUTES, A HIGH SCHOOL STUDENT'S IS (3) MINUTES AND FOR A KINDERGARTNER IT'S 30 SECONDS. YOU DON'T EVEN HAVE THAT MISTER"
- VINCE LOMBARDI

he would die almost immediately. I remember fighting back tears as I watched his press conference as he told the world, "I will attack this like I have attacked my opponents throughout my career, and I'm going to beat this disease."

Before this challenge for Magic, I believed everything that came out of his mouth. He talked of winning championships, and he won 5 NBA titles. But beating the virus that causes AIDS at that time was hard for anyone to believe, except for Magic.

Today Magic is a healthy, vibrant businessman, entertainer, philanthropist, and AIDS spokesperson that touches thousands of people's lives every day. Do you think he would be here if he didn't have a positive mental attitude? I don't think so.

Most people like being around positive people. I know I do. I don't like spending time around negative people or situations because I know there's nothing worth having that comes from negativity. Be the kind of student teachers like and are willing to help. Be the student that other students look up to and want to be like.

Be an example for younger students coming after you to strive to be like. It doesn't cost a thing to put a smile on your face and go to school every day expecting the best.

List 5 things about your attitude that you can improve.

1.

_____

2.

_____

3.

_____

4.

_____

5.

_____

Visualize and write down how much better your life will be when you make these changes.

1.

_____

2.

_____

3.

_____

4.

_____

5.

_____

Chapter 4

Leadership: Do You Lead or Do You Follow?

Leadership is the art of getting someone else to do something you want done because he wants to do it.
~ Dwight Eisenhower

From my earliest childhood memories, I was always a leader. As I stated earlier, a big part of my life has been athletics. When you're always competing, you are forced to make decisions and make them fast. Since I felt comfortable playing anything, I always felt comfortable stepping up and leading every situation I could. People seemed to like following my lead in sports and in school because I was confident I could lead people to do better than they expected.

Being a leader is hard because you have to be different to be effective. Most people don't realize that a lot of successful people in many different areas including politics, education, business, and even sports are the ones who were different or had a hard time fitting in!

We all move to a different beat or have a different song going on in our heads. Going against the grain or standing out in school will sometimes make you an outcast, but as you get older the people who set out to make their own course are rewarded in a number of different ways.

The way our educational system is set up trains us to learn a little about a lot of different subjects, and this allows us to be well rounded. But there are many people like a lot of entrepreneurs who tend to be interested in just a few subjects. They may not be as strong in the overall system of school but they thrive in the areas that interest them.

People like Microsoft founder and owner Bill Gates attended college (Harvard) but knew at an early age exactly what he wanted to do. Most people would argue that leaving a Harvard education behind was not a wise decision, and I would agree with that. But Bill Gates had an idea of what was coming next (computer software—1980s), and he went after it. The rest is history for the world's richest person!

Now I'm not suggesting you don't finish your education, because I know how important my education has been for me. I wouldn't be half the man that I am right now nor had nearly as much success if I had not gone to college. What I am saying is pay attention to your special gift that you have to offer the world, and go after it with everything you have, no matter what others think!

The sports world has more than its fair share of people who were leaders and turned out to be superstars in their sport. One such person who comes to mind is one of the world's greatest boxers, Muhammad Ali!

Ali started out as Cassius Clay, born in Louisville, Kentucky. He was always a smart and charming young man, and for a while he was best known for running his mouth. Cassius, while fighting as an amateur during his teenage years, would go door-to-door telling anyone who would listen what he was going to do to his opponent in his next fight. He was confident and, some say, even cocky, but above it all he made sure that his approach was different. People would come to see him fight if only to see him get beat. But that didn't happen very often.

After winning the gold medal in the Olympics, Clay wanted nothing more than a shot at the heavyweight championship. At the time Sonny Liston, a big, bruising, and intimidating fighter, was the champion. Clay approached him about fighting but was turned down. But did Clay stop when he got the news? Most people would have thought, "Well, I gave it my best shot. I guess I'll just have to wait." But remember, we are talking about going against the grain, being a leader.

" GOD HAS GIVEN EVERYONE THE ABILITY TO DO SOMETHING, ONCE YOU DISCOVER WHERE YOUR ABILITY IS, YOU MUST CONCENTRATE ON DEVELOPING IT" - JESSE OWENS

Clay decided to bother and harass Liston everywhere he went. Clay once used a loudspeaker outside of Liston's Denver home in the middle of the night and screamed from outside, demanding a fight for the title. Clay once saw Liston in a Las Vegas casino and grabbed his dice while Liston was playing and challenged him right there.

Eventually Liston agreed to fight Clay for the title. Cassius Clay lived up to the hype and beat Liston so badly he refused to continue fighting after the 7th round, which Clay predicted! Finally, Clay had the championship. When he was interviewed after the fight, he screamed, "I'm the greatest, I'm the greatest" so loud the interviewer couldn't get a word in.

After the fight, Cassius Clay changed his name to Muhammad Ali and told the world of his new religion, the Nation of Islam. Knowing that people would view him in a negative way, Ali never backed down from his beliefs. During the Vietnam War, Ali refused to be inducted into the Armed Forces because of his religious beliefs. He lost everything from his heavyweight title, money, and his ability to make a living, but he stood strong.

After a few years, the United States Supreme Court ruled in Ali's favor and reinstated him to boxing. Ali went on to have one of the most remarkable boxing careers and is recognized as one of the greatest human beings in the world for his strong beliefs and his stance for peace!

It takes courage to be different and to be a leader, to take a stand-alone from the crowd, but if you are strong enough to weather the storms, you will find success in whatever area you desire.

If you find yourself outside of the main group or looked at as weird by some of your classmates, don't worry. Have confidence in yourself that you are your own person, and stand strong on this belief. Find role models who can help you get closer to your interests.

Unfortunately, we hear examples of teens that have lost their lives because of poor choices involving alcohol and drugs. Some of these decisions are made because of peer pressure or the need to belong. Learn early to be your own person, to stand strong for what you believe in, and people will learn to respect you even if they don't quite understand you.

During my professional basketball career, I was fortunate enough to play overseas in France, Italy, Japan, Spain, and Venezuela along with the NBA. During my travels, I lived among and learned from all types of people. When you surround yourself with people who think differently than you and you have an open mind, you can learn so much more than you would otherwise.

I challenge you to meet someone new or someone from a different "clique" every year you're in school. Don't worry about what other people think. You are trying to be the best you can be, and going against the flow sometimes is necessary to grow. Open your mind to different ideas and different people, and you will be successful!

List 5 leadership qualities you have right now.

1.
2.
3.
4.
5.

List 5 people you feel are leaders, and list the reasons why.

1.
2.
3.
4.
5.

Chapter 5

Networking

"IT'S NOT WHAT YOU KNOW IT'S WHO YOU KNOW"

Since the end of my professional basketball career, I have continued to work in sports. I have done some consulting for other companies that need assistance with sporting events, I have run my own sports events, and I currently work in the sports media field. Currently, I'm a sports reporter for CBS 2 Chicago, color analyst for college basketball on ESPN, and color analyst for the University of Illinois men's basketball on the radio.

During my basketball career, I would do radio and television internships and run basketball camps to get business experience during the off-season. This gave me the work experience I needed to enter the sports media field after my retirement.

But my networking ability, the ability to build personal relationships with people in positions of influence, has been as important if not more important to my success than anything else.

Many people overlook the importance of networking in career advancement. But think of this: If you go for a summer job at McDonald's, the manager is hiring YOU, not what you represent. The manager wants to know what kind of person you are more than your skills, because if he or she can develop trust in you, you will probably be a good employee.

Now using the same example, if the manager is a family friend of yours or you have known the manager for some time, the interview process is not that important because the manager already knows you. People who hire other people WANT to hire people they know!

Put yourself in the situation of being a boss. Would you prefer to hire someone you don't know or someone you have known for a while and you know what to expect from this person? It's the same in the business world.

As a student you may be wondering, this is cool but I'm too young to be worried about networking. Once you're in high school, you need to start the process. Schools have all kinds of people who are there to help you attain your goals and do well in school.

When I was growing up in Carbondale, I had a lot of people--the superintendent, the principal, the school counselor, teachers, coaches, and other parents—to help me on my path. I was recruited by more than 100 colleges and universities around the country, and most of the time college coaches wanted to talk with people other than my high school coaches to find out what kind of person I was.

I developed good relationships with almost everyone I came in contact with, and they would pass on good information to college coaches from different schools. Do you think Lou Henson, the coach of the University of Illinois at the time, would put up with me and offer to pay more than $50,000 for my college education if I was a knucklehead?

My opportunity with CBS started 15 years ago with a letter my father suggested I write to ESPN thanking them for having me on a radio show during one of my college basketball seasons. That letter ended up in the hands of the president of ABC Sports, who just happened to be an alumnus of the University of Illinois. I would write this gentleman every six months or so just to see how he was and to keep him up on my progress. Once I got some experience in the sports media world and an opportunity came up at CBS Chicago, I got the once-in-a-lifetime break because of the relationship I maintained with him over the past 15 years! Thanks, Dennis!

Ask your parents, a teacher, or a school counselor to help you identify people who can help you attain your goals and give you advice and access to information in whatever your area of interest. The beautiful thing about networking is you can make friends for life in a wide range of backgrounds and expertise.

You may be wondering, how do I start networking, where do I begin? Your school and community are two of the best places to start. I was on the basketball team and ran track and cross country in high school. All of these teams have a coaching staff, and I would make sure to put forth my best effort at all times to help my teams win. This showed the coaching staff that I was serious about my commitment to the team, I respected them and my teammates, and I worked hard. This made the coaches' job easier because they knew what to expect from me. They also were more willing to help because I was helping them.

Other areas within the school setting are various student organizations. These provide a perfect setting to establish credibility with other students because of your contribution to the group. Many times your involvement with these groups can result in new friendships that can last a lifetime and possibly help you down the line.

" I COULDN'T HAVE SCORED ONE GOAL WITHOUT MY TEAMMATES. I LOVE THEM AND ALWAYS WILL"
- MIA HAMM

Volunteering in your community is a great way to network. Many of the adults you will come in contact with during community service are some of the most successful and most respected in your community. Giving back to your community is one of the best things you can do to strengthen your ties and relationship with other people you live close to. A commercial may talk about "giving back to make a better place." Well that's not just talk. It's true!

Volunteering gives everyone a sense of community pride and shows the adults in the group that you are a special young person, one they would be willing to help in the future!

Along with these activities, you need to get an address book. Everyone--and I mean everyone--you develop a relationship with should be listed in there. I'm sure some students have Palm Pilots or another type of address book on their phones as well. Whatever you choose to use, understand that it's very important to keep and update contact information for the people you know, because you never know when someone can make the difference in your life.

Always remember, networking is a two-way street. It's not all take and no give. Universal law demands that you give of yourself and you shall receive. Look for ways to help others and be an asset to others. The quickest way to get what you want is to help enough people get what they want first. We are all world citizens, and if we strive to help others before helping ourselves, we can make an incredible impact on our communities. So get out there and find people you can help, and watch your life grow in ways you could not imagine!

List 3 organizations (school or community) that you can be part of and make a difference.

1.

_____

2.

_____

3.

_____

List 3 areas where your personal strengths can be an asset to others.

1.

_____

2.

_____

3.

_____

Chapter 6

Get and Stay in Shape

"If you train hard, you'll not only be hard but hard to beat"
-Herschel Walker

Growing up in Carbondale, Illinois, I had an advantage over many kids from an athletic standpoint because I could run or ride my bike pretty much wherever I wanted. Carbondale is a small college town of about 30,000 people. It's home to Southern Illinois University, which has about 25,000 students, so, as you can see, this was not a big-city atmosphere.

The basketball court where I learned how to play and spent most of my time was about a mile from my house.
Many times I would run while dribbling the basketball on the way there and back. Little did I know at the time that I was establishing a healthy lifestyle that would benefit me long after my playing days were over. It gave me a competitive edge in terms of conditioning that would boost my professional basketball career.

Things were a little bit different then than they are now. There were no computers, no DVDs, and not until I got to junior high school did we enjoy cable TV! Before cable, we had four or five channels--that was it.

Unless we were playing board games like Monopoly, Backgammon, or Scrabble or playing cards, we would be outside doing something physical. I remember riding bikes; playing basketball, baseball, football, soccer, tennis, and golf; running track; swimming; and playing any other sport you can think of. The recreation center on the university's campus was like heaven for my buddies and me. We could go in there and play everything available, and it was the best time because I was spending time with my friends and family and I was doing something healthy.

Unfortunately, young people today have many other things that compete for their attention, and most of them don't require getting off your behind. Technology has been good and bad when it comes to our youth.

With the Internet, X-Box, Playstation, 800 channels on DirecTV, and so on, young people just aren't getting enough exercise, and that's not good. We have seen an alarming rise in juvenile diabetes and obesity that comes from lack of exercise and poor diet.
If young people don't take control over their bodies, we as a country will be looking at some serious health problems in the next 10 to 20 years.

I know it's hard for you young readers to understand the importance of taking care of your bodies. You're young, and your bodies heal quickly when you are hurt, so you move on without a thought. But it will not always be this way. Some of you can eat anything you want and not gain a pound, but it won't always be that way.

I played organized basketball for more than 20 years, from grade school to junior high to high school to college and then professionally. During those 20 years, you couldn't find 100 people in this country who were in better shape than I was. I could run and jump all day long and get up the next day and do it again. I made a living with my body, so I know more than most about this subject.

Even after all the training and playing I've done, my body has started to change. I don't heal as quickly as I once did. It's harder for me now to stay in shape like I was before. I have to watch what I eat now because I can feel it when I don't eat right. So if I can feel a difference even with my long sports career, what do you think 99% of the people--who don't have my background--feel?

" THE FUNDAMENTALS MAY BE THE LITTLE THINGS, BUT USUALLY THEY MAKE THE DIFFERENCE BETWEEN WINNING AND LOSING" - KAREEM ABDUL JABBAR

When you exercise, there's a chemical in your body that goes into your bloodstream called endorphins. This chemical, once released, makes your body feel great, helps you think better, helps regulate your mood, and increases your appetite! The more you move your body and work out, the better you will feel, the better you will perform in the classroom, and the better your mood.

I know when I work out consistently I feel better because I know I'm doing something my body wants. Now my body feels good and I look better because I feel better. My attitude is good because I feel better, and when my attitude is good I achieve more. And since I'm achieving more, it makes me want to work out more so I can continue to achieve what I want. Do you see the cycle?

That's why many of the most successful people find some kind of exercise and they do it consistently. Many of the top CEOs of *Fortune* 500 companies are serious runners, cyclists, tennis players, golfers, rowers, and other high-intensity sports participants. They know that without a physically fit body the mind can only go so far.

You may be wondering, how do I start? I suggest finding something that you really like doing. It could be dancing, skating, cycling, gymnastics, or another sport. Find a friend or two to join you. When you have partners, you can motivate each other. Start off slowly. You need to develop some kind of exercise plan for the rest of your life, so don't kill yourself at the beginning. Experiment with different things so you can find multiple activities to keep you from getting bored. Most importantly, HAVE FUN!

Exercise is not meant to be work. It's supposed to be fun. Enjoy getting out and moving your body. Keep it fun and exciting for you and your friends, and you will notice an immediate change.

If you are already active, great! Keep it that way. The more you can exercise on a regular basis, the better your life will be in so many ways, and you'll feel better during the process.

List 5 physical activities that you like to do.

1.
2.
3.
4.
5.

List 3 people you would like to join you when exercising.

1.
2.
3.

Chapter 7

College: The Best Time of Your Life!

"The most important aspect of college is the social aspect. The people you meet in college will be your friends for life"
Harold Bardo

I had an advantage over most people when I went to college. I basically grew up on the campus of Southern Illinois University. My father was a student athlete there in addition to being a Ph.D. there now, and my mother graduated from there as well. My extended family includes Dr. Seymour Bryson, who played basketball with my father at SIU and is now a dean there. My Uncle Paul and Aunt Carol both work at SIU and have for many years.

When my brother Craig went off to college, I went with my father to take him to Indiana University. I remember being somewhat speechless because of the size and beauty of the campus and being almost scared of Bobby Knight, the head coach of Indiana at the time. We would go to Bloomington sometimes to watch Craig's games, and I would get so excited to be in Assembly Hall with 17,000 screaming fans. These experiences had a long-lasting effect on me.

I remember watching my sister Helen play basketball at John A. Logan Junior College. She was much closer than Craig, so I got a chance to see her go to class, see some of her classmates and teammates, and really see her college experience.

So when it was my turn to go I had all of this firsthand knowledge of what to expect and how I was going to fit in. I didn't have the nervous feeling that most freshmen have when they set foot on campus for the first time. I knew I was going to succeed.

My mother took me to college for the first time, but before we left home, my Dad talked with me about college. I remember him saying to me to do my very best with the books because a college education is the best tool you can start your life off with. He also told me to really get to know my fellow students because the friends you make in school will stay with you the rest of your life.

As I look back 15 years to my college experience, my Dad was right on target. I still call my college roommates almost every week. I met my wife in college. My professional basketball career was enhanced because I played on the "Flyin Illini" team that reached the Final Four and to this day is one of the most exciting in college basketball history. And the knowledge that I received from college still benefits me to this day!

Now I understand that not all people will get a chance to go to college. Some are not prepared mentally for the freedom that comes with college, and others may not learn best in that setting. But for everybody else who can find a way to get there, I would strongly suggest going to college.

You young people today get mixed messages when you see high school phenoms like LeBron James go straight from high school to the NBA. In his case and a few others, I believe he made the right decision. We see musicians who may start out in high school but hit it big and don't think they need the college experience. There will always be exceptions to the rule, but for the majority of young people I strongly suggest the college route.

It doesn't matter if you go to Harvard, the state school in your area, or the community college. I believe everyone who has a chance to go should go.

The benefits of college are obvious. With a college degree, you can start out your adult life with a degree that companies are looking for. But college gives you far more than just the classroom experience.

" YOUR OPPONENT, IN THE END, IS NEVER REALLY THE PLAYER ON THE OTHER SIDE OF THE NET, OR THE SWIMMER IN THE NEXT LANE, OR THE TEAM ON THE OTHER SIDE OF THE FIELD, OR EVEN THE BAR YOU MUST HIGH-JUMP. YOUR OPPONENT IS YOURSELF, YOUR NEGATIVE INTERNAL VOICES, YOUR LEVEL OF DETERMINATION."

- GRACE LICHTENSTEIN

One of my observations as an adult is that no matter how smart you are, if you can't relate and work with other people, you will have a hard time. College gives you this opportunity to meet people with different views and backgrounds and allows you, if you have the right attitude, to grow and learn from others.

College also gives students the kind of freedom that will lead them to be able to be successful once they finish. At the University of Illinois, some students handled the freedom well and others didn't. But even the ones who didn't were protected because it wasn't the working world yet. The mistakes you make in college can be damaging, but the mistakes you make in the adult world can sometimes haunt you the rest of your life!

Time management comes into effect big-time once you're in college. As a student athlete, my time was pretty much taken up with my duties as a member of the basketball team. My typical day went something like this:

8:00 - 8:45am	Breakfast
9:00 - 2:00pm	Classes
2:30 - 5:30pm	Basketball Practice
6:00 - 7:00pm	Training table/Dinner
7:00 - 9:00pm	Study Hall

After study hall, I was usually so tired that all I could do was watch a little TV or study for tests.

But the average student didn't have that kind of schedule and had more flexibility to do social things. I remember students who took classes in mid to late afternoon and sometimes-early evening. As a basketball player, I could never do that because of practice and games.

So you will have to make decisions about your time, which is great training for the work world.

You will have time for everything including social activities, but it's up to you to make the most out of your time, and I don't know a better training ground than college.

Another aspect of college is the social experience. Now imagine there are anywhere from 5,000 to 50,000 young people your age, with no money like you, with the same wants and needs as you, trying to achieve their own goals just like you! There is NO other place like it, nor will you ever be in that kind of situation after college. The opportunity to make friends in college is 100 times better than any other situation you can be in.

With this opportunity comes responsibility as well. On campuses around the country, there are parties almost every night. This is a part of the campus scene and, if done right, can be a great time. But if you allow yourself to be consumed by alcohol and drugs, you are setting yourself up to fail, period!

The influence of alcohol and drugs can alter your thinking, and you can find yourself in dangerous situations. Many times young people experiment with sex under the influence. Sex is not a game; teenagers and young adults account for the majority of new HIV cases in this country. You don't want your life to change forever because of a foolish thing you did after drinking alcohol or taking drugs.

There are far more productive activities on campuses that don't require you to drink to be cool, or to smoke to hang out with the "in" crowd. Remember, this is YOUR life, and if someone else doesn't respect you enough to let you be you, then cut him or her off like a bad habit! Don't worry, you will find other, more positive people to spend your time with.

If you are fortunate enough to receive a scholarship to college, or if your parents can afford to pay your way, be grateful. If you have concerns about finding money for college, talk with your school counselors and ask them to help you find a way to get to college. That's what they are there for--to help you get to your destination. In my experience, if you show enough passion and concern about going to college, the counselors, along with other administrators, will do their best to help you. But you have to make the first move. If you take that first step, you will find many people to assist you.

Our country depends on today's young people being well educated to take the torch and improve on what we have now. So get busy preparing yourself for college. You won't regret it. I promise!

List 3 teachers, counselors, or administrative staff you can talk with about going to college.

1.
2.
3.

Name 3 colleges or universities that you would be interested in attending.

1.
2.
3.

Chapter 8

The Real Deal About Money

There was a time when a fool and his money were soon parted, but now it happens to everybody. Adlai Stevenson.

Every now and then, I get a chance to watch music videos with my 13-year-old son, Stephen Paul. His music of choice is Hip Hop, and I have to admit I love it, too. One thing that has changed since I first watched music videos back in the 1980s is the way the musicians try and show off material things and try to imply they have a lot of money. I'm sure some do, but most of the artists we see only have one or two songs under their belts, so I know they're not rolling in dough.

Shows like "MTV Cribs," "How I'm Living," and "Celebrity Rides" always put the emphasis on living large. These shows highlight the possessions of the young, rich, and famous entertainers and athletes many young people like to watch.

If viewed in a realistic light, I believe these shows can be motivating. But beware of only going after material possessions. Keeping up with the Joneses has gotten many people into financial trouble very quickly!

Saving

My friend and mentor, Cuttie Bacon, states in his book *How To Teach Kids To Be Millionaires* that $1 to $2 a day saved over 40 years will add up to $500,000 with the use of compound interest. This shows that EVERYBODY has the opportunity to become wealthy.

Think about this for a moment. How many times have you spent a couple of dollars on candy, junk food, or gadgets that you stopped using after a few weeks? I challenge you to start thinking long-term and understand that EVERY decision you make with money can make you rich or poor. It's up to you.

Credit Cards

Honestly, if I had my way, credit cards would be illegal! I remember getting my first credit card in college and I thought, "Man, this is cool. Now I can go out and get what I want." But what most teenagers and young adults forget is that you have to pay that money back, with a fee!

If you have a credit limit of $500, that's not your money. The credit card company is loaning you this money whenever you buy something, and the company wants it back with interest. If you read your local newspaper, I guarantee you can find an article in the next week or so talking about people getting into serious debt with credit. Just watch TV long enough, and you will see commercial after commercial telling viewers you can "consolidate your debt into just one easy monthly payment." There are big companies set up *only* because people have abused and continue to abuse credit, so beware!

10% Rule

If you read books by the country's most successful financial authors, one rule that EVERYONE talks about is that to be successful in handling your money, save 10% of everything you make and don't spend it. Just like the example above shows what you can do with a dollar or two every day, just think what your bank account would look like if you could do this.

This technique also teaches you a very good habit of not spending all that you make. Some people even take it a step further and save 10%, tithe or give 10% to their church and live off of the remaining 80%. With these great money habits, you can't help but achieve whatever you desire in the future.

" IT IS AMAZING WHAT CAN BE ACCOMPLISHED WHEN NOBODY CARES ABOUT WHO GETS THE CREDIT"
- ROBERT YATES

All of these ideas are tested over time and work, but you have to make the commitment to see it through. Some of us are born to wealthy parents and have a leg up. Some of us are born into tough economic situations where poverty and scarcity are the norms. But regardless of your situation, as young people you have time on your side. Any consistent effort on your part to take control of your money will result in dreams you can only imagine.

Being wealthy is your birthright, not the exception to the rule!

Write down 3 ways that you can save $1 to $2 a day.

1.

_____

2.

_____

3.

_____

List 3 areas of interest to you that you can turn into a part-time project/job.

1.

_____

2.

_____

3.

_____

Chapter 9

Hard Work: Your Best Friend!

"Sweat plus sacrifice equals success"
Charlie Finley

As I look back on my life growing up, I never really thought about working hard at anything, I just did it. Whether it was in the classroom or sports, I just thought that everyone worked hard and I was no exception. If I were interested in something, I would put my head down and get busy, not really understanding that I was actually working hard toward what I wanted.

I thank my parents for that because they created an environment for my brother, sister, and I in which we expected to work for anything we got. There were no free lunches or handouts; we earned everything we got. As I think back, they must have watched a lot of "Star Wars" sequels because they had the Jedi mind tricks going!

My first experience with people not wanting to work hard for what they wanted happened in college. I met this young man in my freshman year and we became friends. But as the years went on, we started drifting apart because of our belief systems about work.

He was extremely gifted and an outstanding basketball player, but he had a hard time when it came to practice. As long as we were scrimmaging, he was fine. But during the defensive and rebounding drills and the conditioning part of practice, he was not competitive.

Everybody that plays basketball at a competitive level loves to play the game, but there is so much more involved in being a winner. You have to pay the price upfront before you achieve success, and my buddy didn't want to pay the price.

I've always known that I'm not the smartest, fastest, strongest, or even most handsome man, although my mother would argue with you on that one! But I do know that I can study harder to get smarter, I can run more to get faster, I can lift weights to get stronger, and all of this is pure effort and hard work.

Anyone who has had any success in anything will tell you: There is no secret to success. It's believing in yourself, staying focused on what you want, and outworking the competition or holding your own feet to the fire. Nothing else is needed to achieve your goals, just old-fashioned hard work.

That's why earlier in the book I stressed that you need to find your passion or something you love to do because we all have to work at something. Unfortunately, many adults have "settled" into a job or career they don't love or even like sometimes, and they never reach their full potential. If you have to get up and go to work, you should try to make it something you will STAY excited about.

I was very fortunate to have the opportunity to play professional basketball for 10 years. Many men would give body parts in exchange for the chance to do what I have done. I made a living playing a game! When you get older and get more work experience, you will understand how special that is.

But I worked my tail off to get the chance to play professionally. In high school, when everyone else was on Christmas break chillin' at home, I was in the gym running sprints and working with my teammates and playing in holiday tournaments.

" IF YOU EVER WANT TO BE A DECENT PLAYER, YOU HAVE TO LEARN TO USE EACH FOOT EQUALLY WITHOUT STOPPING TO THINK ABOUT IT". - PELE

At Illinois, I remember being close to tears my freshman year because I couldn't go home Christmas Day because we had practice. Knowing everyone was back home having a blast, I had to stay in the hotel after practice and look at my long-faced freshman teammates, who were feeling the same way.

During the summers when everyone else was enjoying the weather, I was running sprints on the football field, lifting weights in the sauna-like weight room, and shooting 500 jump shots a day to work on my game.

In the off season during my professional career, I would do 30 to 60 minutes of cardio work on the treadmill or Stairmaster®, then go to the court and play one-on-one with my workout partners and then work on skill development, then drag myself into the weight room for a 1_-hour session. Then toward the end of the summer, when I was getting close to playing, I added wind sprints on the football field and another playing session in the evenings.

As you can see, I was able to play at that level because I worked my tail off. There are no born players, lawyers, doctors, CEOs, teachers, or accountants--they are MADE. There are no free lunches in the working world--there are leaders (hard workers) and there are followers (doing just enough to get by).

When I talk with young people around the country, I am bothered to see that some have this attitude that someone owes them something. Like someone is supposed to come by and provide you with everything you need to be successful. Or others who feel sorry for them for the situation they are in. I'm here to tell you, "It's not where you are; it's where you're going."

How is it that immigrants from other countries can come here with no English, very little money, and very little knowledge of how things work here? But that doesn't stop millions of people from other countries because they see the streets here in the United States paved with gold! Many of them see opportunity where many Americans don't, and the only difference is they aren't too proud to get down and dirty and work for what they want.

Teenagers in this country have a tremendous opportunity with a global economy, unlimited access to information on the Internet, and technology at your fingertips to do what was once thought impossible. I encourage you to go after what you want with intensity and desire and don't quit until you get it.

List 3 areas of your life that would improve immediately with hard work.

1.

2.

3.

Name 3 people that you admire because of their work ethic.

1.

2.

3.

Chapter 10

You Can't Be It If You Can't See It

"If you can believe it, the mind can achieve it"
Ronnie Lott

I like to use motivational quotes to help me through the day and to help keep me going in tough times. I have seen and read many throughout the years, but this by far is my favorite: "You can't be it if you can't see it." It seems so obvious, but actually it's not.

When I talk with students, I use this quote and then ask them what it means. I get some interesting responses, but very few know exactly what I'm talking about.

My understanding of this quote is, if you can't imagine yourself doing something, if you can't see a mental picture of you being something, it doesn't matter how hard you work--you will NOT achieve it!

Have you ever seen or heard someone interviewed who is at the top of his or her profession? Sometimes the question "How did you make it to this level?" comes up. The response will be, "I used to dream or see myself doing this for as long as I can remember" or "I would watch and imitate this person and see myself doing the same thing."

The power of visualization in unlimited. This great gift that all of us have can be used in a number of different ways. Children use it to imagine themselves a superhero, flying in to save the day. Teenagers use it to imagine being on stage performing like their favorite music artist. Adults don't use it as much, but the ones who do imagine themselves reaching levels within their profession or personal life that they once thought impossible.

There is an exercise I encourage all young people to try. When I was eight years old, my father was a professor in educational psychology--that means he understands how the mind works. He understood and taught others why people act and learn the way they do. So I now know that my brother, sister, and I were his little experiments.

" SPORTS DO NOT BUILD CHARACTER... THEY REVEAL IT" - JOHN WOODEN

One day I told my Dad while watching the NBA on television that I would love to play in the NBA someday. I would watch Magic Johnson, Larry Bird, Isaiah Thomas, and my favorite--Dr. J, or Julius Erving. I was amazed by their ability and how hard their teams used to play. I loved watching the rivalries like Philadelphia versus Boston or the Lakers versus the Celtics. Every weekend during basketball season, if we weren't doing something as a family, I was in front of the TV watching the drama unfold.

My Dad told me to take the poster of Dr. J, cut his head off the poster, and put a picture of me smiling where Dr. J's head was. I laughed at the thought, but since my Dad told me to do it I did it.

My Mom got a head shot of me smiling, and I put it on Dr. J's body.

My Dad told me to look at the picture every morning and night and work on my game, and I would make it to the NBA! Well I would look at the poster in the morning when I woke up and in the evening before I went to bed. At the time, I remember my left hand was weaker than my right when I dribbled and passed the basketball.

Soon after I altered the poster, I noticed my left hand got better. Then I finally beat a guy in my neighborhood that I could never beat. I swear I ran all the way home from the court, and I don't remember my feet touching the ground once!

I kept this up, and before I knew it, I was in high school and people were starting to take notice of my game. I was invited to the BC all-star camp. At the time, this was one of the best basketball camps in the country. Many future NBA players were at the camp. I had read about some of the guys before I got there like Sean Elliott and J. R. Reid but never thought the day would come when I would be playing against them. I was the unknown guard from the small town that had a great camp and made the all-star team.

I remember my Dad asking me how well I did and I said, "I did all right." A month later, when letters started flowing in from colleges around the country, my Dad came back and said, "You must have done better than okay!"

I kept looking at the picture and working on my game, and I entered my senior year as one of the top 50 players in the country. Soon after that, I received a scholarship to the University of Illinois. After a very successful college career, I was drafted in the second round of the 1990 NBA draft!

That's why I know this technique works. I looked at that poster from the age of 8 to 18 and I got to my destination. This works for anything you are trying to achieve. No matter if you want to be a lawyer, politician, computer specialist, or manager, it works. You have to find a picture of someone doing what you want to do, take the head off of the picture, and put a picture of your head on top. Then look at it morning and night, put in the necessary work, and you will get there.

Final Thought

You are the captain of your own ship--not your parents, teachers, or other friends, but you. Take the principles in this book and apply them consistently. Involve your parents, teachers, and any other adults you trust to help you come up with a plan to use these ideas in your daily life. You can create any future you want. Don't let anyone tell you anything different.

"In order to do something you've never done, you've got to be someone you've never been"! -- Les Brown

ORDER INFORMATION

"How To Make The League Without Picking Up The Rock"

Students Will Learn:

- Why EVERYONE needs a backup plan
- How to set and achieve goals to ensure success
- Why networking is so important
- The Real Deal about money
- A positive mental attitude is a must

Email - Stephen@StephenBardo.com

Schools or anyone ordering large quantities, please call
(312) 869-9757

Title	Copies	Price
How To Make The League Without Picking Up The Rock	_____	$11.95
Shipping/Handling ($4.00)		_____
TOTAL		_____

Speaking Engagements

To have Stephen Bardo speak at your school, conference, or company please contact him at the information below:

(312) 869-9757
Email: Info@StephenBardo.com
Website: www.StephenBardo.com

I would love to hear. Write or email me at the information above and let me know how this book has helped you.
Thanks for your support!!!!